■ Codes

Code	Meaning	Code	Meaning
—	Cursor Position	[HRt]	Hard Return
[-]	Hyphen	[Hyph]	Hyphenation
-	Soft Hyphen	[HZone]	Hyphenation Zone
[Adv]	Advance	[→ Indent]	Indent
[Block]	Beginning of Block	[→ Indent ←]	Left/Right Indent
[Block Pro]	Block Protection	[Italc]	Italics
[Bold]	Bold	[Just]	Justification
[Box Num]	Caption in Graphics Box	[L/R Mar]	Left and Right Margins
[Cell]	Table Cell	[← Mar Rel]	Left Margin Release
[Center]	Center	[Note Num]	Footnote/Endnote Number
[Center Pg]	Center Page Top to Bottom	[Outln]	Outline (attribute)
[Cntr Tab]	Centered Tab	[Paper Sz/Typ]	Paper Size and Type
[Col Def]	Column Definition	[Pg Num]	New Page Number
[Col Off]	End of Text Columns	[Rgt Tab]	Right-Aligned Tab
[Col On]	Beginning of Text Columns	[SPg]	Soft Page Break
[Comment]	Document Comment	[SRt]	Soft Return
[Date]	Date/Time Function	[Subscpt]	Subscript
[Dec Tab]	Decimal-Aligned Tab	[Suppress]	Suppress Page Format
[Dorm HRt]	Dormant Hard Return	[Suprscpt]	Superscript
[DSRt]	Deletable Soft Return	[T/B Mar]	Top and Bottom Margins
[Endnote]	Endnote	[Tab]	Left-Aligned Tab
[End Opt]	Endnote Options	[Tab Set]	Tab Set
[Fig Box]	Figure Box	[Tbl Box]	Table Box
[Fig Opt]	Figure Box Options	[Tbl Opt]	Table Box Options
[Flsh Rgt]	Flush Right	[Text Box]	Text Box
[Font]	Base Font	[Txt Opt]	Text Box Options
[Footnote]	Footnote	[Und]	Underlining
[Ftn Opt]	Footnote Options	[Undrln]	Underline Spaces/Tabs
[HLine]	Horizontal Line	[Usr Box]	User-Defined Box
[HPg]	Hard Page Break	[Usr Opt]	User Box Options
		[VLine]	Vertical Line
		[W/O]	Widow/Orphan

▪ Teach
▪ Yourself
▪ WordPerfect 5.1

14 *Customizing WordPerfect with the Setup Feature and Macros* **318**

Taking a Look at the Setup Menu	320
Creating Automatic Backup Files	322
Timed Backups	322
Creating an Auxiliary Backup-File Directory	324
Original Backups	326
Retrieving Backup Files	328
Changing Default Formatting Codes	329
Changing Units of Measurement	332
Setting Up WordPerfect to Use Long File Names	335
Creating Macros	339
Named Macros	339
Alt Macros	341
Temporary Macros	343
Using Macros	344

15 *Creating Form Letters with the Merge Feature* **346**

Creating the Primary File	348
Creating the Secondary File	352
Merging the Primary and Secondary Files	355
Merging Directly to the Printer	357

16 *Working with Graphics* **362**

Creating Horizontal and Vertical Lines	364
Drawing Horizontal Lines	364

- *Teach*
- *Yourself*
- *WordPerfect 5.1*

Contents at a Glance

Introduction   xix

1 Getting Started   1

2 Basic Editing Techniques   32

3 More Editing Tools   58

4 Line Formatting Techniques   80

5 Paragraph Alignment Techniques   110

6 Page Formatting Techniques   134

7 Formatting Characters and Using Fonts   160

8 Expanding Your Editing Power with the Block Feature   188

9 Using Headers and Footers, Footnotes and Endnotes   204

10 Using Document Summaries and Comments, Search and Replace, the Speller, and the Thesaurus   226

11 Getting the Most from Your Printer   256

12 Working with Columns   268

13 Creating and Working with Tables   286

14 Customizing WordPerfect with the Setup Feature and Macros   318

15 Creating Form Letters with the Merge Feature   346

16 Working with Graphics   362

A Formatting Floppy Disks   390

B Installing WordPerfect 5.1   398

C Using a Mouse with WordPerfect 5.1   428

Index   437

- *Teach*
- *Yourself*
- *WordPerfect 5.1*

▪ Teach
▪ Yourself
▪ WordPerfect® 5.1

Jeff Woodward

San Francisco ▪ Paris ▪ Düsseldorf ▪ Soest

Teach Yourself book concept: David Kolodney
Acquisitions Editor: Dianne King
Series Editor: Cheryl Holzaepfel
Copy Editor: Richard Mills
Technical Editor: Nick Dargahi
Word Processor: Deborah Maizels
Book Designer: Ingrid Owen
Desktop Publishing Operators: Daniel Brodnitz, Charles Cowens, Ingrid Owen
Production Editor: Carolina L. Montilla
Screen Graphics: Delia Brown
Indexer: Julie Kawabata
Cover Designer: Archer Design
Cover Photographer: David Bishop

■ *Acknowledgments*

Teach Yourself WordPerfect 5.1 is the next evolutionary development in the SYBEX visual guide series. A great deal of effort by some very fine individuals has resulted in the book you see before you. Many of these people quietly sat in small cubicles and contributed their important part to a large and complex project. Their names are unknown to me, but I could not have produced this work without their help. I would like to express my gratitude for their hard work; thank you all, very much.

Thanks again to Cheryl Holzaepfel, my series editor, for her continually perceptive guidance and helpful support through yet another visual guide project.

Thanks go to Richard Mills, who did an excellent job as my copy editor. With his help I was able to stay organized and keep the manuscript accurate.

I am very appreciative of Dianne King, Acquisitions Editor, and Dr. Rudolph Langer, Editor-in-Chief, for their continued support.

I want to especially thank Hannah Robinson, Vice President of Marketing, for her fine work in supervising the marvelous design of the book cover.

My congratulations and thanks go to WordPerfect Corporation for continuing to refine WordPerfect into the finest word processor on the market today.

Jeff Woodward
17 April 1990
Los Angeles, California

Contents at a Glance

Introduction   xix

1 Getting Started   1

2 Basic Editing Techniques   32

3 More Editing Tools   58

4 Line Formatting Techniques   80

5 Paragraph Alignment Techniques   110

6 Page Formatting Techniques   134

7 Formatting Characters and Using Fonts   160

8 Expanding Your Editing Power with the Block Feature   188

9 Using Headers and Footers, Footnotes and Endnotes   204

10 Using Document Summaries and Comments, Search and Replace, the Speller, and the Thesaurus   226

11 Getting the Most from Your Printer   256

12 Working with Columns   268

13 Creating and Working with Tables   286

14 Customizing WordPerfect with the Setup Feature and Macros   318

15 Creating Form Letters with the Merge Feature   346

16 Working with Graphics   362

A Formatting Floppy Disks   390

B Installing WordPerfect 5.1   398

C Using a Mouse with WordPerfect 5.1   428

Index   437

■ Table of Contents

Introduction   *xix*

A Quick Tour through the Chapters   xx
Computer Basics   xxi
     About Software   xxi
     About Hardware   xxii
     Caring for Floppy Disks   xxiv
     DOS—The Disk Operating System   xxiv
     Understanding Computer Memory   xxv
     Keeping Track of Your Data   xxv
Using the Keyboard   xxvi
     Special Keys   xxviii
     Function Keys   xxix
     The Numeric Keypad   xxx
Using a Mouse   xxxi
Using WordPerfect's Menu System   xxxii
A Closer Look at the Visual Approach   xxxv
Before You Begin   xxxix

1   *Getting Started*   *1*

Starting WordPerfect from a Hard Disk   2
Starting WordPerfect from Floppy Disks   5
Creating a Sample Document   7
Moving the Cursor   9
Inserting Text   11
Deleting Text   13

Viewing the Document before Printing   15

Printing the Document   18

Saving Your Document and Exiting WordPerfect   23

Getting Help   26

2 Basic Editing Techniques

Basic Editing Techniques   32

Retrieving a Saved Document   34

   Retrieving by File Name   34

   Retrieving a File with List Files   35

Creating Soft and Hard Page Breaks   40

Advanced Cursor Movement   43

   Moving One Word at a Time   43

   Moving to the Beginning and End of a Line   44

   Moving to the Beginning and End of a Document   44

   Moving One Page at a Time   45

   Moving to the Bottom and Top of a Page   46

   Moving One Screen at a Time   46

   Scrolling through Text with the Mouse   47

Advanced Deletion Techniques   48

   Deleting Words   49

   Deleting Lines   49

   Deleting to the End of a Page   50

Restoring Deleted Text   51

Saving an Edited Document   53

   Saving and Returning to the Document   54

   Saving and Exiting from WordPerfect   55

3 More Editing Tools   **58**

Working with Hidden Codes   60
    Editing in Reveal Codes   62
Splitting and Combining Paragraphs   65
Repeating Keystrokes   67
Working with Multiple Documents   70
    Displaying Two Documents in Windows   71
    Clearing the Windows   74
Changing the Date Format   76

4 Line Formatting Techniques   **80**

Setting Line Margins   82
    Editing Margin Codes   85
    Deleting Margin Codes   87
Setting Line Spacing   89
Working with Tabs   90
    Deleting Tab Stops and Setting New Ones 91
    Using Tab Stops   94
    Changing Tab Stops   95
Hyphenating Words   99
    Keyboard Hyphenation   99
    Automatic Hyphenation   102
Justifying Text   103
Eliminating Widows and Orphans   106

5 Paragraph Alignment Techniques — **110**

Indenting Paragraphs — 112
    Indenting from the Left Margin — 112
    Indenting from the Left and Right Margins Simultaneously — 115
    Creating Hanging Indents — 118
Centering Text — 121
    Centering New Text — 122
    Centering Existing Text — 123
    Centering Text at the Cursor Location — 126
Aligning Text Flush with the Right Margin — 127
    Flush-Right Alignment of New Text — 127
    Flush-Right Alignment of Existing Text — 129

6 Page Formatting Techniques — **134**

Setting Top and Bottom Margins — 136
Defining Forms and Selecting Paper Size and Type — 138
    Defining Forms — 139
    Selecting Paper Size and Type — 144
    Selecting Sizes without Defining Forms — 146
Numbering Pages — 149
    Suppressing Page Numbers — 153
    Setting New Page Numbers — 156

7 Formatting Characters and Using Fonts — **160**

Typing Boldfaced and Underlined Characters — 162

Deleting Boldface and Underline 163

Boldfacing and Underlining Existing Characters 165

Choosing an Underline Style 167

Changing between Uppercase and Lowercase 169

Changing the Size and Appearance of Your Text with Fonts 170

Changing Base Fonts 170

Selecting Fonts 172

Changing the Size of a Base Font 178

Changing the Size of Existing Characters 182

Changing the Appearance of Characters 183

Combining Character Styles 185

8 Expanding Your Editing Power with the Block Feature

188

Deleting, Moving, and Copying Blocks 190

Deleting Blocks 190

Moving Blocks 192

Copying Blocks 194

Moving and Copying Blocks for Future Use 195

Moving and Copying Text between Documents 197

Printing Blocks 199

Saving Blocks 200

Appending Blocks to Existing Files 201

9 Using Headers and Footers, Footnotes and Endnotes

204

Creating Headers and Footers 206

Creating a Header 206

Creating a Footer 209

Editing and Deleting Headers and Footers 212

Working with Footnotes and Endnotes 214
Creating Footnotes 215
Editing Footnotes 216
Formatting Footnotes 218
Creating and Editing Endnotes 220
Formatting Endnotes 222

10 Using Document Summaries and Comments, Search and Replace, the Speller, and the Thesaurus **226**

Creating Document Summaries and Comments 228
Creating a Document Summary 228
Creating a Document Comment 234
Using Search to Find and Replace Data 236
Searching Forward for Text or Codes 236
Searching Backward through a Document 239
Replacing Text 241
Using the Speller and the Thesaurus 244
Spell-Checking a Document 244
Creating a Supplemental Dictionary 249
Using Wildcards 251
Using the Thesaurus 252

11 Getting the Most from Your Printer **256**

Printing from Disk 258
Setting Margins for Binding 260
Selecting the Number of Copies 261

Selecting Graphics and Text Print Quality   262
Controlling Your Printing Jobs   264

12 *Working with Columns*   **268**

Creating Newspaper Columns   270
Creating Parallel Columns   274
Changing Existing Column Definitions   279
Editing and Moving the Cursor between Columns   282

13 *Creating and Working with Tables*   **286**

Creating the Table Structure   288
Changing the Table Structure   292
   Joining Cells   292
   Changing Table Size   294
   Changing Line Size and Type   296
Placing Text in the Table   302
   Typing Text in a Cell   302
   Retrieving a File into a Cell   304
Working with Numerical Entries   307
   Creating Formulas   307
   Copying Formulas to Other Cells   310
   Recalculating Formulas   311
Formatting Cells   313

14. Customizing WordPerfect with the Setup Feature and Macros — 318

Taking a Look at the Setup Menu — 320
Creating Automatic Backup Files — 322
Timed Backups — 322
Creating an Auxiliary Backup-File Directory — 324
Original Backups — 326
Retrieving Backup Files — 328
Changing Default Formatting Codes — 329
Changing Units of Measurement — 332
Setting Up WordPerfect to Use Long File Names — 335
Creating Macros — 339
Named Macros — 339
Alt Macros — 341
Temporary Macros — 343
Using Macros — 344

15. Creating Form Letters with the Merge Feature — 346

Creating the Primary File — 348
Creating the Secondary File — 352
Merging the Primary and Secondary Files — 355
Merging Directly to the Printer — 357

16. Working with Graphics — 362

Creating Horizontal and Vertical Lines — 364
Drawing Horizontal Lines — 364

Drawing Vertical Lines	368
Creating Boxes for Text and Graphics	372
Creating a Box Style	373
Placing Text in Boxes	376
Importing WordPerfect Graphics into a Document	382
Importing Graphics from Other Programs	389

A Formatting Floppy Disks   390

Formatting Your Floppy Disks	392
Dual Floppy-Disk Computers	392
Hard Disk Computers	394

B Installing WordPerfect 5.1   398

Installation on Dual Floppy Disks	400
Installation on a Hard Disk	416

C Using a Mouse with WordPerfect 5.1   428

Hints for Installing Your Mouse	430
Setting Up Your Mouse	433
Index	437

■ *Introduction*

Welcome to *Teach Yourself WordPerfect 5.1*, a guide to the powerful tools available in WordPerfect 5.1. Whether you are new to computerized word processing, or are experienced with other versions of WordPerfect, or would like to make the transition from another word processing program to WordPerfect 5.1, then you will find this book an excellent place to begin.

You'll notice that this book looks quite different from most computer books. Its unique visual approach enables the book itself to reflect as closely as possible the actual experience of using WordPerfect 5.1 at the computer. *Teach Yourself WordPerfect 5.1* is an efficient and effective tool if you want to learn word processing as you work at the computer, but don't really want to read pages and pages of text to accomplish this goal. The exercises are not lengthy, providing the most benefit in the least amount of time.

Why, you ask, is this book any better than the documentation that came with the WordPerfect 5.1 program? The documentation, excellent as it is, is primarily a reference manual, an alphabetical listing of the many functions of the program. While this can be very helpful, *Teach Yourself WordPerfect 5.1* is designed to be a learning aid to guide you through the basic features of WordPerfect. You are directly involved from the first moment, activating keystroke commands and creating sample documents. Each step is followed by an actual picture of what appears on your monitor. You will be surprised at how fast and easy it is to get up and running with WordPerfect 5.1.

Although there are several versions of WordPerfect and different models of computers they work with, this book concerns itself with version 5.1 for the IBM PC/XT, /AT, and PS/2 family of computers and those that are compatible with them.

There have been many powerful enhancements made in this latest release of Word-Perfect, and it is still compatible with earlier releases of WordPerfect. This compatibility enables you to transfer WordPerfect 4.2 and 5.0 files to WordPerfect 5.1. Also, files created in version 5.1 can be saved in the 4.2 and 5.0 formats.

A Quick Tour
■through the Chapters

Before starting with Chapter 1, there are a few preliminary tasks that you'll need to take care of. You should have WordPerfect 5.1 properly installed in your computer. Appendix B at the end of the book has instructions for completing this task.

Once you've completed the installation, you're ready to start with Chapter 1. The best way to use this book is to follow the tutorial exercises from beginning to end. However, if you want to skip ahead for information about a particular feature, feel free to do so, substituting one of your own documents in place of the one used in the exercise.

Chapter 1 guides you through the procedures for starting your computer and the WordPerfect 5.1 program. You will create, edit, save, and print your first document.

Chapters 2 and 3 introduce you to more advanced editing features that will help you speed up your work. You'll discover advanced methods of moving the cursor, deleting text, and working with WordPerfect codes.

Chapters 4 through 7 teach you how to format your documents to achieve the look you desire. A few of the things you'll learn how to do are changing margins and tabs, justifying and hyphenating text, numbering pages, aligning text, and selecting different styles of type.

Chapter 8 shows you how to delete, copy, save, move, and print blocks of text— extremely helpful techniques when editing documents.

Chapters 9 through 11 present some powerful, specialized features of Word-Perfect. You will learn how to create headers and footers, footnotes and endnotes, how to use the WordPerfect dictionary and thesaurus, and how to control your printer.

Chapter 12 guides you through the intricacies of creating multicolumn documents. If you work with newsletters, this chapter is invaluable.

Chapter 13 teaches you how to use the Tables feature to create a table.

Chapter 14 gives you information about customizing the start-up settings of the WordPerfect program. You also learn how to create macros, simple programs that automatically execute formatting operations that you perform regularly.

Chapter 15 teaches you how to use WordPerfect's merge feature to create form documents, such as form letters used in mass mailings.

Chapter 16 introduces you to the basics of WordPerfect's desktop publishing feature. You will learn how to create horizontal and vertical lines and how to import graphics into your documents.

Appendix A guides you through the procedures for formatting new floppy disks, which you must do before you can record information on them.

Appendix B shows you how to use WordPerfect's installation program to install WordPerfect on floppy disks or on a hard disk.

Appendix C provides instructions for using a mouse with WordPerfect. You will find this appendix useful if you have never used a mouse before.

Inside the covers of this book you will find material that provides you with instant reference to information on cursor movement, menu selections, and key combinations needed to activate WordPerfect's many features; you will also find a list of the most common WordPerfect formatting codes.

■ Computer Basics

Before you begin working with WordPerfect 5.1, there are a few things you should know about your computer. In this section you'll learn about hardware and software, floppy disks, and a little about how your computer uses DOS, its operating system.

About Software

The term *software* refers to the many programs that can run on your computer. Examples of software are WordPerfect, Lotus 1-2-3, dBASE IV, and DOS. The variety and amount of software on the market is practically endless—everything from word processing and business applications to banner makers and games is available.

Software comes to you on one or more floppy disks. If you have a hard disk (see "About Hardware" below for descriptions of hard and floppy disks), you will most likely copy your programs from the floppy disks to the hard disk. If you have a computer with only floppy drives, you must use the program floppy disks each time you run the program.

About Hardware

The main computer components that you need to operate WordPerfect are a monitor and display card, a printer, disk drives, and the computer itself. This equipment is referred to as computer *hardware*.

Monitors

A monitor is the screen on which you view your document. Monitors come in a multitude of models that vary in shape, size, and quality of resolution. You may have a monochrome, composite, or color monitor. WordPerfect will run on all of them. However, some features may be disabled, such as View Document on a monochrome, text-only video setup (MCGA).

The most common monochrome monitors display images in green or amber on a black background.

Composite monitors are also monochrome, but they can display lighter shades of green or amber. This gives you shading variations that can be adjusted in the same way that color differences can be adjusted on color monitors. For instance, the setting for yellow displays a lighter shade of amber or green than the setting for red.

Color monitors can display at least 16 colors. WordPerfect allows you to customize the background and foreground colors to suit your tastes.

Display Cards

The display card is an important part of your monitor/computer system. It links the computer with the monitor, allowing program information and the images that you create at the keyboard to be processed and displayed on the monitor screen. Each type of monitor requires its own display card, so make sure your system is set up properly. This is very important if you purchase your monitor and computer separately and connect them yourself.

The display card also affects the monitor's *resolution*—the clarity of the display images. The degree of resolution can be an important consideration if you plan on working with sophisticated graphics.

Disk Drives

Disk drives operate the hard or floppy disks that contain your software applications. (These disks also store the documents you create.) There are two types of disk drives—floppy disk drives (5¼" or 3½" diameter) and hard disk drives.

If your system has two floppy drives, they are most likely stacked on top of each other with horizontal drive slots. The top drive is called drive A; the lower drive is called drive B.

Hard drives do the same job as floppy drives, with some differences. The disks used in hard drives are thicker and harder, hold a great deal more information, and transfer data more quickly. The hard drive is usually called drive C and is usually mounted internally in the computer. (External hard drives are also available.) So, if your system has both a hard and a floppy drive, you have an A and a C drive.

Printers

WordPerfect can work with hundreds of different printer models. There are basically three types of printers: dot-matrix, daisy-wheel, and laser printers. Word-Perfect works well with all three types.

Dot-matrix printers print text or graphics by grouping hundreds of small ink dots into the correct shape or design. The print from these printers is not usually high-quality, although several expensive brands come close to letter-quality print; consequently, documents printed on dot-matrix printers are often rough drafts, lists, memos, and low-quality graphics.

There are two types of letter-quality printers: daisy-wheel and laser. A daisy-wheel printer, like a conventional electric typewriter, uses a plastic print element called a daisy wheel to print characters. These printers are usually slow, noisy, and limited to printing text. Laser printers are more expensive, but they can print both letter-quality text and high-quality graphics, and do it quietly and quickly.

Caring for Floppy Disks

Care must be taken when using your floppy disks, especially with those disks that contain WordPerfect and your operating system. It is important that you make backup copies of all your software. With WordPerfect, you have to install the program on a second set of floppy disks or on a hard disk, leaving the original disks as a backup. If your working disks become unusable for any reason, simply install the program on another set of serviceable disks. (See Appendix B, "Installing WordPerfect 5.1"). Take care never to bend your disks, expose them to magnetic fields, or subject them to extreme heat or cold, cigarette smoke, or any chemicals that give off vapors. Store your disks in plastic or cardboard boxes.

To insert a floppy disk in a horizontal drive, open the drive latch and slide the disk into the slot with the label facing up and the write-protect notch facing left. The write-protect notch is the rectangular cutout on one edge of the floppy disk. On a 3½" floppy disk, the write-protect notch is the small square window with the tab that can be moved back and forth. High-density 3½" disks have two write-protect tabs. Be careful not to touch the portion of the disk exposed by the long oval slot; if you do, you may lose valuable information stored on the disk. Be sure to close the drive latch after inserting the floppy disk in the drive.

DOS—The Disk Operating System

DOS can be mystifying if you're new to computers. I'll try to shed a little light on this subject and put you at ease.

The DOS system works as a master program that controls the flow of information between the separate components of your computer system, such as between the computer and the storage disks, and between the computer and the printer. DOS is a software program that must be loaded each time you start the computer in order to run WordPerfect or any other software program. If you have a hard disk, you have to install DOS on your hard disk, if the computer manufacturer hasn't already done so. Once installed, it is automatically loaded every time you start the computer. If you have floppy drives, you must insert a disk with DOS recorded on it in a floppy disk drive before you start the computer. This start-up procedure is known as *booting up*.

Understanding Computer Memory

Computers have two types of memory—temporary and permanent—and there are important differences between them. As a beginner, you may think the information you type into the computer is there forever, to be called upon whenever you need it—type a document, turn off the machine, and return later for editing. I'm afraid it's not as easy as that.

The area of the computer where your newly entered data is initially stored is called RAM (random access memory) and is a temporary storage area. If you turn off your machine, or if there is a power failure of some sort, you immediately lose all the data stored in RAM, because the data is only temporarily stored there until you record it permanently. Until the data is recorded, or *written,* on a disk, it can be lost.

Why have temporary memory? Why not have it recorded permanently as you enter the data in the computer? Recording information on a floppy or hard disk is a physical process and is much slower than manipulating the data electronically, which is what RAM is used for. The continuous recording of data on a floppy or hard disk as you worked would be very time consuming and would defeat one of the main benefits of having a computer—speedy processing.

The objective, of course, is to have your hard-wrought data stored permanently for future use. Putting data into permanent memory is the recording of the data on a floppy or hard disk. This procedure is called *saving.* You can compare it to making a recording of a favorite song from the radio. Once you listen to the song it's gone, but if you record it on a tape, you can listen to it as often as you want. So, if you are wise, you will save your data on a disk often while you work so that you will not lose valuable information.

Keeping Track of Your Data

Thinking in terms of location is important when working with computer data. Knowing how to manipulate data is important, but you must also know *where* the information is to be saved, retrieved, copied, moved, and so on. If you have a dual floppy-disk system, the choices are fairly clear; your documents are located on disks in either the A or B drive. If you have a hard disk drive, all your information is usually on drive C, because it can hold much more data than a floppy disk.

Because drive C has a vast amount of storage space, the space is usually organized into directories, in which you save similar types of documents and which make it easier to find files. A *file* is data that is saved, as a unit, and has a specific name assigned to it. A hard drive can hold literally hundreds of files. Knowing which directory your file is located in, and how to get there, is vital to the efficient use of your computer.

As you work through the exercises in this book, you will learn how to tell the computer where you want files saved and how to find files once you've saved them in a directory.

Try to visualize the monitor as your work area and the A, B, and C drives as file drawers in an electronic file cabinet. Your files are located within these file drawers. Some of the files are organized into separate groups called *directories*. When you want to bring a file to your work area (monitor), you have to tell the computer to look in the correct file drawer (the A, B, or C drive) and directory. The route the computer follows to find the file is a called a *path*. For example, if you gave your computer the path C:\WP51\JONES.LTR to find a file, the computer would go to drive C (*C:*), then to the WordPerfect 5.1 directory (*WP51*), and retrieve the file named JONES.LTR. If you wanted to store the file in that location, you would type in this same path when you saved the file.

Talking about this subject and understanding it are two different things. Don't be concerned; as you work through the exercises in this book and tackle your own projects, you will soon become comfortable with these ideas. A light bulb will click on in your mind, and you will understand these ideas perfectly.

■*Using the Keyboard*

The keyboard that you have for your computer works much like a conventional typewriter, with several important differences. The illustration shows three common styles of keyboards. There are some keys that work exactly the same as on

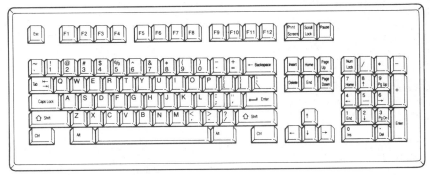

IBM PC/AT

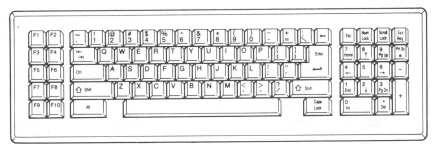

IBM PC/XT

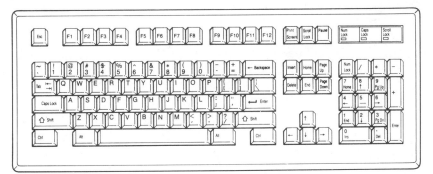

IBM PS/2

a typewriter, but when used in combination with other keys, they perform special functions. In addition to these special keys, there are function keys that are not found on typewriters. Just as a pilot must be familiar with the instrument panel and controls of any new airplane he or she flies, so must you become familiar with the keyboard, for that is where you control WordPerfect 5.1.

Special Keys

Look at your keyboard and locate the following keys:

TAB · · · · · The Tab key. In WordPerfect, TAB moves the cursor to the next tab stop. When used with SHIFT, it becomes a margin release key.

↵ · · · · · The Enter key (also called the Return key). It is one of the most frequently used keys on the keyboard. You use it to end paragraphs, insert blank lines within text, and enter certain commands for execution by WordPerfect. When you see the ↵ symbol in this book, press the Enter key.

BKSP · · · · · The Backspace key. You use it to delete an unwanted character to the left of the cursor, *not* to move backward through the text.

INS · · · · · The Insert key. It is used to switch between the Insert and Typeover modes. In the Insert mode (active at start-up), existing characters move to the right to make room for the new ones that you type. In the Typeover mode, the new characters you type replace the existing ones.

SHIFT · · · · · The Shift key is used to create uppercase letters; it works just like the Shift key on a typewriter. When used in conjunction with the function keys, the Shift key also executes certain editing functions.

ALT · · · · · The Alt key is used in conjunction with the function keys to execute certain editing functions.

CTRL   The Control key. Like the Alt and Shift keys, it is used in conjunction with the function keys.

ESC   The Escape key. It is used by WordPerfect as the Repeat key, automatically repeating characters and commands. You can also cancel formatting operations when you change your mind midstream.

DEL   The Delete key. When you press this key, you erase the character or code that is at that cursor position.

↑   The cursor arrow keys. On some keyboards, a second set of these keys is found on the numeric keypad on the 2, 4, 6, and 8 keys. (The *cursor* is the small flashing underline that indicates where each character you type will appear.) These keys allow you to move the cursor throughout your document without disturbing the text.

↓

←

→

Function Keys

The function keys are labeled F1 through F10 or F12, depending on which style of keyboard you are using. They are located along the top of the keyboard on the enhanced style, or in two columns on the left side of the keyboard on the older styles. No matter the location, they perform the same tasks.

These keys have been programmed to perform the many complex tasks of WordPerfect. Certain functions are performed by pressing the function keys by themselves; other functions are accomplished by pressing the function keys in conjunction with the Shift, Alt, and Ctrl keys. You will find that you'll remember the key combinations you use regularly. For those key combinations that you use less frequently and may need to look up, WordPerfect provides a Help feature that will tell you the command and key combination needed to activate a feature.

WordPerfect also includes two templates with its documentation; the templates fit over the function keys on the enhanced and older-style keyboards. The templates are color-coded, with the WordPerfect features printed on the template in the color that corresponds to the special key to be pressed, according to this scheme:

Template Color	Corresponding Special Key
Red	CTRL
Green	SHIFT
Blue	ALT

For example, suppose you want to use the Format command. *Format* is printed in green on the template next to F8, so to activate the feature, you press the Shift key and hold it down while you press the F8 key. Function-key commands printed in black on the template are pressed alone, not in combination with any special key.

The Numeric Keypad

The numeric keypad is located on the right side of your keyboard. It is useful when you work with a lot of numbers. It is easier to manipulate the number keys from the keypad than it is to reach up for the numbers along the top of the keyboard.

To activate the numeric keypad, you simply press the Num Lock key. An indicator in the lower-right corner of the WordPerfect screen flashes when Num Lock is on. On some keyboards, a light on the Num Lock key itself or in the upper-right corner of the keyboard indicates that the numeric keypad is in use. The arrow keys on the numeric keypad (numbers 2, 4, 6, and 8) do not move the pointer or cursor when Num Lock is turned on; instead, the numbers are displayed on your screen. To deactivate the numeric keypad, you press the Num Lock key again. The screen indicator stops flashing and the indicator lights, if you have them, go out.

▪ *Using a Mouse*

There are two tools you can use to interact with WordPerfect: the keyboard and the mouse. You read about the keyboard in the previous section. Let's take a look at how to use a mouse with WordPerfect.

A mouse is a small, hand-held object connected to your computer by a thin cord. If you have a mouse connected to your system, it will be sitting next to your computer. Mice are usually rectangular or oval and may have one, two, or three buttons. Look at the drawing. If you use your imagination, the body of the device resembles the body of a mouse, and the cord looks like its tail.

The mouse is used to move a small rectangular pointer that appears on your monitor screen and, in effect, does the same job as the cursor movement keys on your keyboard, only faster. The mouse pointer is moved across the screen by sliding the mouse over a flat surface (some mice are moved over a special, light-sensitive pad); the pointer moves in the same direction as the mouse. When WordPerfect is in graphics mode, the pointer takes the shape of an arrow. (See Appendix C for helpful hints on installing and setting up your mouse.)

You can use the mouse to place the cursor in another location, scroll through a document, and select menu options. To do so, you *click, double-click,* and *drag* the mouse. *Click* means to press and immediately release the mouse button.

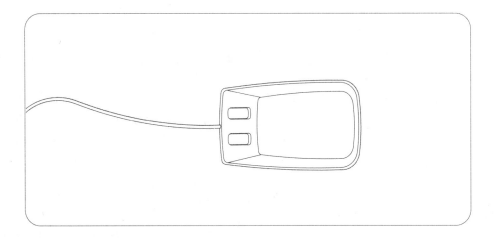

Double-click means to rapidly click the mouse button twice, within a double-click interval (set by default at $7/10$ of a second). *Drag* means to press the mouse button, hold it down, and move the mouse pointer.

Using
■*WordPerfect's Menu System*

WordPerfect provides a very useful pull-down menu system. You can activate this menu system from the keyboard or with the mouse. This system performs the same functions as the keyboard function keys do, without requiring you to memorize the function-key sequences—very helpful for those features you seldom use.

Many of the exercises in this book instruct you to "select" menu items. To activate the WordPerfect main-menu bar from the keyboard, you press [ALT] [=] (press and hold down [ALT], then press the equal sign); with the mouse, click the right mouse button. The main-menu bar is displayed across the top of your screen:

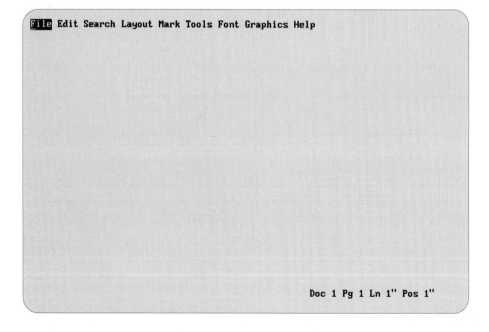

You can select an option from the main menu in one of three ways:

- Move the mouse pointer to the desired option and click the left button.
- Using the arrow keys, move the highlight to the desired option and press ⏎.
- Press the boldface letter in the menu option's name—for example, the *S* in **S**earch or the *O* in F**o**nt.

When you select an option on the main-menu bar, a pull-down menu appears from which you can select a WordPerfect feature:

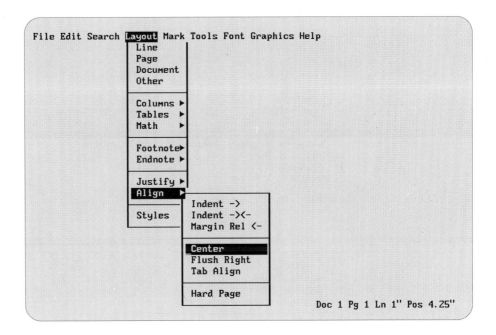

Selecting some pull-down menu options displays a submenu that offers another level of options. Those pull-down menu options that display submenus have a triangle (▶) pointing to the right.

Once displayed, there are four ways to select an option from a pull-down menu:

- When you select an option from the main-menu bar, do not release the left mouse button. Instead, hold it down and drag the mouse pointer

across the menu list to the option you want, then release the button to activate the option.

- Move the mouse pointer to the option you want, then click the left
  mouse button to activate the option.
- Use the arrow keys to move the highlight to the option you want, then
  press ⏎ to activate the option.
- Press the boldface letter for the option you want.

When you select a pull-down menu option, you will often be offered another,
more detailed, menu:

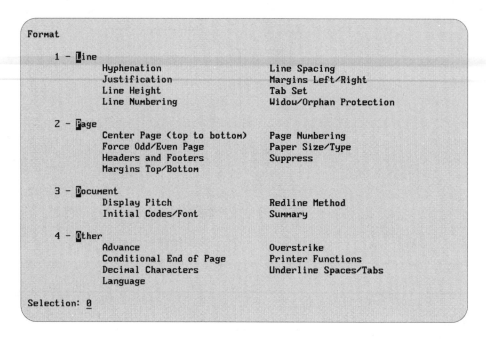

```
Format

   1 - Line
            Hyphenation                Line Spacing
            Justification              Margins Left/Right
            Line Height                Tab Set
            Line Numbering             Widow/Orphan Protection

   2 - Page
            Center Page (top to bottom)   Page Numbering
            Force Odd/Even Page           Paper Size/Type
            Headers and Footers           Suppress
            Margins Top/Bottom

   3 - Document
            Display Pitch              Redline Method
            Initial Codes/Font         Summary

   4 - Other
            Advance                    Overstrike
            Conditional End of Page    Printer Functions
            Decimal Characters         Underline Spaces/Tabs
            Language

Selection: 0
```

To select an option from this type of menu, place the mouse pointer on the option
name and click the left mouse button, or press the number or boldface letter for
the option.

If you use the function keys instead of the main-menu bar and pull-down menus,
you will see the type of detailed menu displayed above or a *prompt* or *selection
line*. A prompt appears in the lower-left corner of the screen and offers you a **Y**es